Pebble® Plus

Animal Offspring

Dogs and Their Puppies

Revised Edition

by Linda Tagliaferro

CAPSTONE PRESS
a capstone imprint

Pebble Plus is published by Capstone Press,
1710 Roe Crest Drive,
North Mankato, Minnesota 56003
www.capstonepub.com

Library of Congress Cataloging-in-Publication Data
Names: Tagliaferro, Linda, author. Title: Dogs and their
puppies : a 4D book / by Linda Tagliaferro. Description:
Revised edition. | North Mankato, Minnesota : Capstone
Press, a Capstone imprint, [2018] | Series: Pebble plus.
animal offspring | Includes bibliographical references
and index.
Identifiers: LCCN 2017037870 (print) | LCCN 2017052293
(ebook) | ISBN 9781543508628 (eBook PDF) | ISBN
9781543508222 (hardcover) | ISBN 9781543508345 (pbk.)
Subjects: LCSH: Puppies—Juvenile literature. | Dogs—
Juvenile literature.
Classification: LCC SF426.5 (ebook) | LCC SF426.5 .T34
2018 (print) | DDC 636.7/07—dc23 LC record available at
https://lccn.loc.gov/2017037870

Editorial Credits
Gina Kammer, editor; Sarah Bennett, designer;
Morgan Walters, media researcher;
Katy LaVigne, production specialist

Photo Credits
Shutterstock: Anna Goroshnikova, right 21, Anna
Hoychuk, 15, Burry van den Brink, 19 , Christian Mueller,
Cover, Fernando Castelani, right 20, left 21, framsook,
5, Grigorita Ko, 3, 17, Kristin Castenschiold, 7, Nadya
Chetah, 9, Nixx Photography, left 20, Sarune Kairyte, 11,
Stephen Coburn, 13

Note to Parents and Teachers

The Animal Offspring set supports national science
standards related to life sciences. This book describes and
illustrates dogs and their puppies. The images support
early readers in understanding the text.
The repetition of words and phrases helps early readers
learn new words. This book also introduces early readers
to subject-specific vocabulary words, which are defined
in the Glossary section. Early readers may need assistance
to read some words and to use the Table of Contents,
Glossary, Read More, Internet Sites, Critical Thinking
Questions, and Index sections of the book.

Table of Contents

Dogs

Dogs are mammals.
Young dogs are
called puppies.

Male and female dogs mate.

Female dogs give birth

to a litter of puppies.

Puppies

Puppies cannot see
or hear until they are
about ten days old.

Puppies sleep most of the time. Puppies get tired from playing.

Puppies drink milk

from their mother

for about five weeks.

Growing Up

Puppies can eat dog food when they are about six weeks old.

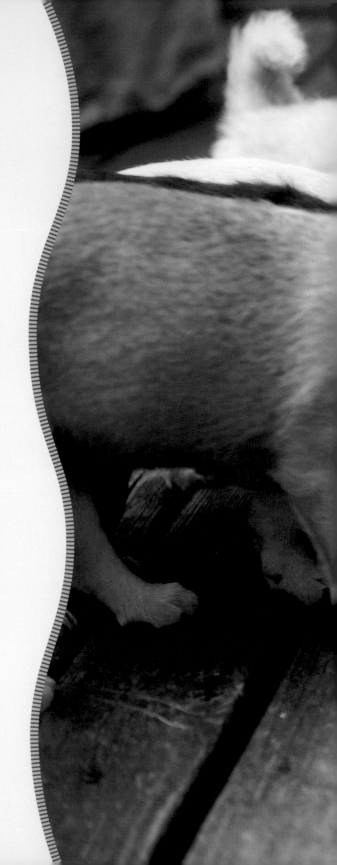

Puppies jump on and play with each other. They chew toys.

Puppies become adults
after one to two years.

Watch Dogs Grow

birth

adult after
about two years

21

Glossary

adult—an animal that is able to mate

litter—a group of puppies born at the same time to the same mother; dogs usually have litters of four to six puppies

mammal—a warm-blooded animal that has a backbone; most mammals have hair or fur; female mammals feed milk to their young

mate—to join together to produce young

Read More

Carr, Aaron. *Dogs.* Science Kids: Life Cycles. New York: AV2 by Weigl, 2016.

Lynch, Annabelle. *Dogs and Puppies.* Animals and Their Babies. Mankato, Minn.: A+ Smart Apple Media, 2017.

Swinney, Nicola Jane. *My Little Book of Dogs and Puppies.* New York: Sandy Creek, 2016.

Internet Sites

Use FactHound to find Internet sites related to this book.

Visit *www.facthound.com*

Just type **9781543508222** and go.

 Check out projects, games and lots more at
www.capstonekids.com

Critical Thinking Questions

1. What are puppies like right after they are born?

2. What is the word used for a group of puppies born at the same time?

3. How do puppies change as they grow into dogs?

Index